Beyond Transient Harmony

Building Your Living Framework

A Workbook for Creating Your Own Philosophical-Spiritual Framework

Author's Note

This workbook was born from the closing invitation of *Transient Harmony*—to take the journey of soul-discovery and begin crafting your own conscious framework.

Within these pages, you are invited to give shape to what you have discovered, to design the language, principles, and practices that reflect your truest self. Let this be the place where awareness becomes architecture.

Frameworks are not cages for belief, but blueprints for becoming.

Beyond Transient Harmony: Building your Living Framework: A Workbook for Creating Your Own Philosophical-Spiritual Framework
 ISBN: 979-8-9941132-2-6

Cover design by Braddon Damien White
 Interior design by Braddon Damien White

First Edition

Published by BDW Press

Printed in the United States of America

For information, visit: www.transientharmony.com

Contents

Introduction to the Workbook

This workbook is not about completing assignments. It is about creating something that is uniquely yours.

Transient Harmony offered one vision of a philosophical–spiritual framework: a way of navigating the journey of life through cosmology, metaphysics, ethics, and practice. The *Work-Along Workbook* invited you to pause, reflect, and live into those ideas for yourself.

Now, the path turns outward—and inward again. This workbook is not about absorbing another framework, but about becoming the architect of your own.

Think of this as a set of tools and open pages for design. Here you will:

- **Survey the land** → explore the beliefs and frameworks you were born into or have borrowed along the way.
- **Draft a blueprint** → sketch the elements of a framework that resonate with your soul.
- **Raise the structure** → weave those elements into a living system that reflects your values and aspirations.
- **Move in and live it** → identify practices and commitments that make the framework real in daily life.
- **Return and remodel** → revisit your framework over time, refining it as you grow.

Your first framework draft may be simple, even borrowed in places. That is not only acceptable—it is expected. Over weeks, months, or even years, you will return to it, reshaping, rearranging, and refining until it feels like home.

The aim is not perfection. The aim is to stand before what you have created and feel proud—not of the product alone, but of the soul you are becoming through the process.

Let this workbook be your lantern and your sketchbook, your compass and your blueprint. Return to it whenever new resonance stirs, whenever old beliefs fall away, whenever you are ready to remodel the home of your becoming.

Welcome to the work of building your living framework.

How to use this Workbook

This is not a book to be read once and placed back on the shelf. It is a space for drafting, sketching, reflecting, and returning. Think of it as your architectural notebook for the soul. A few guiding notes before you begin:

1. There is no timeline

Some may sketch their first framework in a matter of weeks. For others, this process may unfold across months or years. Both are valid. This is not about speed; it is about honesty and resonance.

2. This is version one

What you write here will not be final. Your framework will evolve as you do— remodeled, expanded, refined. Treat every page as a *first draft* that you can revisit later.

3. The process matters as much as the product

The act of reflecting, defining, and writing is part of the transformation. Even if your framework feels incomplete, the soul you are becoming through this work is the deeper outcome.

4. Follow the stages

The workbook will guide you through a process:

- **Learning the Elements** → what every framework typically includes, and why.
- **Surveying the Land** → mapping your inherited and borrowed beliefs.
- **Drafting the Blueprint** → sketching your framework across essential domains.
- **Raising the Structure** → weaving the parts into a whole and naming it.
- **Living Into It** → identifying practices that bring it alive in daily life.
- **The Return Journey** → revisiting, refining, and versioning your framework.

5. Keep it yours

The questions and templates are here to guide you, but the framework that emerges is yours alone. You may rename elements, adapt exercises, or skip sections that do not resonate.

6. Write, sketch, and imagine freely

This space is not for polished essays. Use it as you would a sketchbook—notes, diagrams, symbols, or fragments are welcome. Let form follow feeling.

When you have completed your first pass through these pages, pause and honor it. You will not be finished—but you will have begun. And that beginning is everything.

Setting Your Intention

Before drawing blueprints or laying foundations, every architect begins with a vision. This is your chance to pause and name the orientation you want to carry into the process of creating your own framework.

This workbook will not ask you to finish quickly or to get everything "right." Instead, it will ask you to begin. To trust that the first sketches of your framework, however incomplete, carry the seeds of something lasting.

Use the prompts below as a compass for your starting point. Write as much or as little as you feel called to. There are no correct answers—only the truth of where you stand right now.

Why am I choosing to create my own conscious framework at this point in my life?

_____

_____

_____

_____

_____

_____

_____

_____

_____

_____

_____

What do I hope to discover, define, or strengthen as I work through these pages?

_____

_____

_____

_____

_____

_____

_____

_____

_____

_____

_____

_____

_____

_____

_____

_____

_____

_____

_____

_____

_____

_____

_____

_____

What values, principles, or qualities do I want to carry into this creative process?

_____

_____

_____

_____

_____

_____

_____

_____

_____

_____

_____

_____

_____

_____

_____

_____

_____

_____

_____

_____

_____

What beliefs, habits, or expectations am I ready to release as I begin?

_____

_____

_____

_____

_____

_____

_____

_____

_____

_____

_____

_____

_____

_____

_____

_____

A word, phrase, or symbol that captures the spirit of my intention:

_____

_____

When you reach the later pages of this workbook, you will return to these intentions. You may find they have shifted, deepened, or expanded. That evolution is part of the process.

This is your first step in building a framework that reflects the soul you are becoming.

With your compass set, we now begin the learning stage — exploring the essential elements that form the architecture of every enduring framework.

Part I: Learning the Elements

Before you begin designing your own framework, it helps to understand the essential elements that give any philosophical–spiritual framework its strength. Think of these as the beams and supports that allow your framework to stand tall and endure the test of time. Every tradition, from the Stoics to Taoism, from organized religions to personal philosophies, like Transient Harmony, addresses these domains in some way. You are free to rename them, reshape them, or even combine them—but knowing what they are ensures your framework will be well-rounded and resilient.

1. Cosmological Understanding

The Great Question: *Where do we come from? What is the nature of reality?*

Every framework begins with a worldview. It might be scientific, mystical, religious, or poetic. What matters is not that you answer every cosmic mystery, but that you hold a perspective large enough to give meaning to your life.

Without a cosmology, our framework risks becoming rootless; with it, we see ourselves as part of something greater.

Notes / First Impressions:

_____

_____

_____

_____

_____

_____

_____

_____

_____

_____

_____

_____

_____

_____

_____

_____

_____

_____

_____

2. Metaphysical Foundation

The Great Question: *What unseen structures or principles shape existence?*

Metaphysics explores what lies beneath the surface of daily experience. It could be laws of energy, cycles of time, spiritual realms, or inner dimensions of consciousness. Your metaphysical lens provides texture to your cosmology—it explains how the unseen connects to the seen.

Notes / First Impressions:

_____

_____

_____

_____

_____

_____

_____

_____

_____

_____

_____

_____

_____

_____

_____

_____

_____

_____

3. The Nature of Human Experience

The Great Question: *What does it mean to be human?*

A framework must speak to our lived reality—our bodies, emotions, thoughts, relationships, and mortality. This domain invites you to define how you see human nature: our strengths, our struggles, our potential, and our limits.

Notes / First Impressions:

_____

_____

_____

_____

_____

_____

_____

_____

_____

_____

_____

_____

_____

_____

_____

_____

_____

_____

_____

_____

4. Navigation Principles (Your Pillars or Cornerstones)

The Great Question: *What guides my choices and actions?*

Every framework needs principles that function like a compass. These might be virtues, values, or "pillars." They don't tell you what to do in every situation, but they orient you toward integrity, presence, and alignment when the path is unclear.

Notes / First Impressions:

_____

_____

_____

_____

_____

_____

_____

_____

_____

_____

_____

_____

_____

_____

_____

_____

_____

_____

_____

5. Epistemological Approach

The Great Question: *How do I know what is true or trustworthy?*

Epistemology is about knowledge and wisdom. Do you trust intuition, reason, tradition, lived experience, or all of the above? This element matters because it determines how you discern between noise and guidance, illusion and insight.

Notes / First Impressions:

_____

_____

_____

_____

_____

_____

_____

_____

_____

_____

_____

_____

_____

_____

_____

_____

_____

_____

_____

6. Ethical Framework

The Great Question: *How then shall I live?*

No framework is complete without ethics—the principles that govern how we treat others, ourselves, and the world. Ethics are not just abstract values; they shape real choices and ripple into community, relationships, and society.

Notes / First Impressions:

_____

_____

_____

_____

_____

_____

_____

_____

_____

_____

_____

_____

_____

_____

_____

_____

_____

_____

_____

7. Community & Collective Experience

The Great Question: *How do I relate to others and contribute to the whole?*

Humans do not live in isolation. Every framework must address how we live together—whether in family, society, or humanity at large. This includes community, service, responsibility, and resonance with the collective.

Notes / First Impressions:

_____

_____

_____

_____

_____

_____

_____

_____

_____

_____

_____

_____

_____

_____

_____

_____

_____

_____

_____

8. The Transformative Journey

The Great Question: *How do I grow, change, and evolve?*

A living framework acknowledges transformation. We are not static beings; our souls evolve through cycles of challenge, learning, and renewal. Your framework should hold space for growth and for becoming.

Notes / First Impressions:

_____

_____

_____

_____

_____

_____

_____

_____

_____

_____

_____

_____

_____

_____

_____

_____

_____

_____

9. Practical Integration

The Great Question: *How do I bring my framework into daily life?*

No philosophy endures if it lives only in words. Practical integration is about practices—reflection, rituals, habits, physical disciplines—that make your framework embodied and alive. This is where ideas meet lived experience.

Notes / First Impressions:

_____

_____

_____

_____

_____

_____

_____

_____

_____

_____

_____

_____

_____

_____

_____

_____

_____

_____

_____

_____

You now have a sense of the essential elements. Some will resonate strongly with you; others may feel less urgent right now. That is natural. These domains will become the "rooms" of your framework, but how you decorate them—what language you use, what values you place inside—will be entirely your own.

NOTES

Use this page to capture insights or sketches as you begin imagining your own framework.

Part II: Surveying the Land

Before an architect draws blueprints, they first survey the land. They look at the terrain, note what's already there, and decide what to keep, move, or build upon. In the same way, before creating your framework, you need to see clearly the beliefs, systems, and influences that already shape you.

This is not about judgment—it's about awareness. What you see here will become the foundation you choose to keep, reshape, or release.

Exercise 1: Belief Inventory (Conditioned Framework)

We are all born into frameworks—family, culture, religion, education, society. Some beliefs may still serve you; others may feel outdated or constraining.

Take time to surface these "inherited structures." Write freely. You may discover layers you hadn't consciously noticed before.

Prompts:

- What did I learn growing up about success, failure, or purpose?
- What beliefs about love, relationships, or community were handed down to me?
- What was I taught about the divine, the cosmos, or the unseen?
- Which of these beliefs still resonate? Which feel limiting or untrue?

Space for Reflection:

Use the area below to write freely as you explore the beliefs and frameworks that have shaped you.

_____

_____

_____

_____

_____

_____

_____

_____

_____

_____

_____

Exercise 2: The Resonance Log

Along your journey—through *Transient Harmony*, other traditions, or personal experiences—you've encountered ideas that resonated. They stirred something in you. This log helps you capture those sparks and begin to author them in your own words.

Prompts to get started:

- What concepts or practices from Transient Harmony resonated most deeply with me?
- What wisdom from other philosophies, traditions, or teachers has stayed with me?
- What life experiences of my own have felt like lessons or truths worth carrying forward?

The Spark (quote/idea/practice)	The Essence (what it means to me)	My Principle (rephrased in my words)

As you revisit this log throughout your journey, notice how your "Principles" begin to form the language of your personal framework.

Exercise 3: Keep, Reshape, Release

Now that you've surfaced both inherited beliefs and resonant sparks, it's time to sort them. This is the moment where surveying begins to move toward design.

Instructions:

- Review your Belief Inventory and Resonance Log.
- Place each item into one of three columns:
  - **Keep** → This resonates strongly as-is.
  - **Reshape** → This holds truth, but I want to define it in my own language.
  - **Release** → This no longer serves me.

Keep	Reshape	Release

You've now completed your survey. You know the lay of the land—the inherited terrain, the resonances that call to you, and the structures you want to keep, reshape, or release.

From here, we move into **Part III: Drafting the Blueprint**, where you begin sketching your own framework across the essential domains.

NOTES

Use this space to capture insights, patterns, or realizations that surfaced while surveying the landscape of your beliefs and resonances. What surprised you? What felt ready to release — or ready to build upon?

Part III: Drafting the Blueprint

Now that you've surveyed the land, it's time to begin sketching the first drafts of your framework. Think of this as drawing blueprints: rough, flexible, and open to revision.

This is not your final framework. These are your **first sketches**—lines on paper that can be redrawn as you grow. Remember: a blueprint is not the house itself, but a guide for what may be built.

For each element of a framework, you'll find:

- **Guiding Questions** → invitations to explore.
- **Framework Sketch Space** → where you begin defining your own.
- **Living Into the Blueprint** → prompts that help you consider how this piece might shape your daily life.

1. Cosmological Understanding

The Great Question: *Where do I believe we come from, and how do I see my place in the cosmos?*

Guiding Questions:
- What do I believe about beginnings, endings, and cycles?
- Do I view the cosmos as random, ordered, divine, alive, mechanical—or something else?
- Where do I feel most connected to the vastness of existence?

Framework Sketch Space: Space for writing/sketching symbols/diagrams

Living Into the Blueprint: How does holding this cosmological perspective change the way I live daily life?

_____

_____

_____

_____

_____

_____

_____

_____

_____

_____

_____

_____

_____

_____

_____

_____

_____

_____

_____

_____

_____

2. Metaphysical Foundation

The Great Question: *What unseen structures shape reality?*

Guiding Questions:

- What principles or forces do I believe operate beyond the visible world?
- Do I believe in soul, energy, or other layers of existence?
- How do I understand time, cycles, or destiny?

Framework Sketch Space: space for defining metaphysical principles

Living Into the Blueprint: How does this foundation help me interpret challenges, synchronicities, or mysteries?

_____

_____

_____

_____

_____

_____

_____

_____

_____

_____

_____

_____

_____

_____

_____

_____

_____

_____

_____

_____

_____

_____

3. The Nature of Human Experience

The Great Question: *What does it mean to be human?*

Guiding Questions:

- How do I view the relationship between body, mind, emotion, and soul?
- What is the role of limitation, impermanence, and suffering?
- What do I believe is possible for human growth?

Framework Sketch Space: space for definitions, notes, diagrams

Living Into the Blueprint: How does this view of humanity influence how I treat myself and others?

_____

_____

_____

_____

_____

_____

_____

_____

_____

_____

_____

_____

_____

_____

_____

_____

_____

_____

_____

_____

_____

_____

_____

4. Navigation Principles (Your Pillars or Cornerstones)

The Great Question: *What principles orient me when I don't know what to do?*

Guiding Questions:

- What values feel most central to how I want to live?
- If I had to name 3–5 "pillars" that guide me, what would they be?
- How do I know when I am aligned—or misaligned—with them?

Framework Sketch Space: space for naming and describing each pillar

Living Into the Blueprint: Which area of my life right now most needs the guidance of these pillars?

_____

_____

_____

_____

_____

_____

_____

_____

_____

_____

_____

_____

_____

_____

_____

_____

_____

_____

_____

_____

_____

5. Epistemological Approach

The Great Question: *How do I know what is true or trustworthy?*

Guiding Questions:

- Where do I find wisdom—reason, intuition, tradition, lived experience?
- How do I distinguish between fear and clarity?
- What sources of knowledge do I trust most?

Framework Sketch Space: space for writing/diagramming sources of knowing

Living Into the Blueprint: How does this approach shape how I make decisions or interpret guidance?

_____

_____

_____

_____

_____

_____

_____

_____

_____

_____

_____

_____

_____

_____

_____

_____

_____

_____

_____

_____

_____

_____

_____

6. Ethical Framework

The Great Question: *How then shall I live?*

Guiding Questions:

- What responsibilities do I believe I hold toward others, the world, and myself?
- How do I define integrity, compassion, justice, or stewardship?
- How do I want my choices to ripple outward into the collective?

Framework Sketch Space: space for values, ethical commitments, practices

Living Into the Blueprint: How do I want to practice these ethics in one concrete area of life right now?

_____

_____

_____

_____

_____

_____

_____

_____

_____

_____

_____

_____

_____

_____

_____

_____

_____

_____

_____

_____

_____

_____

7. Community & Collective Experience

The Great Question: *How do I relate to others and contribute to the whole?*

Guiding Questions:

- What role does community play in my life?
- How do I balance individuality with belonging?
- What do I believe is my contribution to the collective?

Framework Sketch Space: space for reflections, notes, diagrams

Living Into the Blueprint: What is one step I can take to live more consciously in community this month?

_____

_____

_____

_____

_____

_____

_____

_____

_____

_____

_____

_____

_____

_____

_____

_____

_____

_____

_____

_____

_____

8. The Transformative Journey

The Great Question: *How do I grow, change, and evolve?*

Guiding Questions:

- How do I understand the process of transformation?
- What stages, cycles, or practices support my growth?
- How do I hold challenges as part of my soul's curriculum?

Framework Sketch Space: space for reflections or personal model of transformation

Living Into the Blueprint: Where do I sense myself in the process of transformation right now?

_____

_____

_____

_____

_____

_____

_____

_____

_____

_____

_____

_____

_____

_____

_____

_____

_____

_____

_____

_____

_____

9. Practical Integration

The Great Question: *How do I embody my framework in daily life?*

Guiding Questions:

- What rituals, habits, or practices help me stay aligned?
- How do I connect big ideas to small daily choices?
- What physical, emotional, or spiritual practices root my framework in lived reality?

Framework Sketch Space: space for defining practices, schedules, rituals

Living Into the Blueprint: What is one small daily action I can commit to that expresses my framework?

_____

_____

_____

_____

_____

_____

_____

_____

_____

_____

_____

_____

_____

_____

_____

_____

_____

_____

_____

_____

_____

You now have a rough draft of your framework across all essential domains. This is your **blueprint**—not final, not polished, but enough to see the outline of what you are building.

Next, in **Part IV: Raising the Structure**, you will begin weaving these elements into a coherent whole, giving it shape, name, and form.

NOTES

Use this space to sketch, refine, or expand on ideas that emerged as you began drafting your first blueprint. Capture patterns, phrases, or visual symbols that seem to define the shape of your framework. What feels clear? What still needs more exploration?

Part IV: Raising the Structure

You've drawn the first drafts of your framework. Now it's time to step back and begin shaping it into a whole. Just as an architect moves from rough sketches to a structure that can be walked through, you will now begin weaving your framework together so it feels like something you can inhabit.

Remember: this is still a first version. You are not locking yourself into permanence—you are giving your framework enough form that you can begin to live in it.

Exercise 1: Naming Your Framework

Names carry power. A name is both a declaration and an invitation. It doesn't need to be clever or final—it simply needs to feel authentic in this moment.

Prompts:

- What words, images, or symbols capture the essence of what I've written so far?
- If my framework were a house, what would I call it?
- What name or phrase makes me feel both proud and at peace when I speak it aloud?

Reflections: space for writing/sketching

Exercise 2: Identifying Your Cornerstones

Just as Transient Harmony is built around Four Pillars, your framework may have its own set of guiding cornerstones. These are the non-negotiable principles that hold everything else in place.

Prompts:

- Looking back across my blueprint, which 3–5 principles feel most essential to my soul?
- If everything else were stripped away, what truths would I still want to stand on?
- What practices or images might symbolize each cornerstone?

Reflections: space for listing and describing each cornerstone

Exercise 3: Sketching Your Framework Map

Frameworks are easier to live into when we can see them at a glance. This exercise invites you to create a one-page "map" of your system. It can be words, symbols, diagrams, or images—whatever feels natural.

Prompts:

- How do the different domains (cosmology, ethics, practices, etc.) connect with one another?
- What image or structure best represents the whole? (a tree, a wheel, a spiral, a house, etc.)
- How can I visualize my framework in a way that helps me remember and live it?

Reflections: use this space for your framework map

Exercise 4: Living Into the Structure

Now that your framework has form, pause to reflect on what it asks of you. Raising the structure is not only about design—it's about beginning to inhabit it.

Prompts:

- Which part of my framework feels strongest and most ready to live into?
- Which part feels like an aspiration—something I want to grow into more fully?
- What is one practice I can begin today that brings this framework to life?

Reflections: space for writing

_____

_____

_____

_____

_____

_____

_____

_____

_____

_____

_____

_____

_____

You now have a name, cornerstones, and a map of your framework. It may still feel rough—that's good. You have raised the structure. It stands tall enough for you to begin moving through it.

Next, in **Part V: Practice and Embodiment**, you will explore what it means to *move in*—to make your framework a lived reality, not just an idea on paper.

NOTES

Use this space to refine and organize the elements of your framework as they begin taking clearer form. Capture insights about how your principles relate to one another, how they balance, and what structure feels most natural and true to you.

Part V: Practice and Embodiment

A framework is not complete until it is lived. Raising the structure is only the beginning; now you move in and make it a home. This part invites you to identify practices, rhythms, and commitments that bring your framework to life in daily experience.

These practices don't need to be grand or elaborate. What matters is that they align with your framework and help you live into it, little by little, day by day.

Exercise 1: Daily Anchors

Your framework will be most alive when woven into the small rhythms of each day.

Prompts:

- What small practice can open and close my day in alignment with my framework?
- Which moments in my daily routine could become reminders of my framework?
- How might I turn ordinary tasks into sacred rituals?

Integration Notes or Living Insights: space for writing/sketching

Exercise 2: Weekly or Seasonal Rhythms

Some practices require a longer rhythm—weekly reflections, seasonal rituals, annual resets. These provide opportunities to pause, zoom out, and realign.

Prompts:

- What day of the week could I dedicate to reflecting, journaling, or meditating on my framework?
- What seasonal or annual rituals would help me honor cycles of growth and change?
- How might I use natural markers (moon phases, equinoxes, birthdays, anniversaries) as times of reflection?

Integration Notes or Living Insights: space for writing/sketching

Exercise 3: Framework in Action

Living your framework means more than reflection—it's expressed through choices, relationships, and service.

Prompts:

- How do I want my framework to shape the way I relate to others?
- Where in my professional life do I want to express my framework more fully?
- How do I want my framework to ripple outward into community and the world?

Integration Notes or Living Insights: space for writing/sketching

Exercise 4: Growing Into It

Your framework will always be larger than your current self. That's the point—it calls you forward. This exercise helps you see where the growth edges are.

Prompts:

- Which part of my framework do I feel most ready to embody right now?
- Which part feels aspirational, asking me to stretch or grow?
- How can I show myself compassion as I live into this vision gradually?

Integration Notes or Living Insights: space for writing/sketching

To practice your framework is to become it. These anchors, rhythms, and commitments are how you move from paper to presence.

Next, in **Part VI: The Return Journey**, you will learn how to revisit your framework over time—remodeling, refining, and expanding it as your life unfolds.

NOTES

Use this space to record experiences, observations, or adjustments as you begin living into your framework. What principles felt natural to embody? Which ones stretched you or revealed areas for refinement? Let these reflections guide your ongoing practice.

Part VI: The Return Journey

A framework is never finished. It is alive, just as you are. What you have written in these pages is not a final product but a **first version**—a framework strong enough to stand, yet open enough to grow.

Just as a home is remodeled over time—new rooms added, walls repainted, spaces reshaped—your framework will change with you. Returning to it is not a sign of failure; it is the mark of an honest, evolving life.

Exercise 1: Version 1.0 Reflection

Pause and honor what you have created here.

Prompts:

- As I look at this first version of my framework, what am I most proud of?
- What part of it feels most alive and resonant right now?
- What part feels like a starting sketch I want to refine later?

Integration Notes or Living Insights: space for writing/sketching

Exercise 2: Six-Month Check-In (or anytime)

Come back to this workbook after six months—or whenever you feel ready—and revisit your framework with new eyes.

Prompts:

- What parts of my framework have I been living into most naturally?
- Where have I noticed growth or unexpected transformation?
- What beliefs, practices, or principles need remodeling now?

Integration Notes or Living Insights: space for writing/sketching

Exercise 3: Version 2.0 Blueprint

Each return is a chance to redraw the blueprint. Use this space to sketch the next version of your framework—whether it's a small refinement or a major renovation.

Integration Notes or Living Insights: space for diagrams, notes, new pillars, etc.

Exercise 4: Ongoing Reminders

Your framework is not just something to revisit in writing—it can also live in small reminders that travel with you.

Prompts:

- What word, phrase, or symbol from my framework can I carry as a daily reminder?
- How might I display my framework in a way I see often—a journal cover, wall art, or digital background?
- Who might I share parts of my framework with, to help me live into it more fully?

Integration Notes or Living Insights: space for writing/sketching

This is not the end of your framework. It is the beginning of a lifelong process of refinement, remodeling, and deepening. Each time you return, you will find both the framework and yourself transformed.

Your framework is not a static system—it is a living companion. May it guide you, challenge you, and remind you of the soul you are becoming.

NOTES

Use this space to explore how your framework is weaving into daily life. Notice moments where your beliefs, choices, and actions feel aligned — and where they still feel separate. What practices, reminders, or shifts help you live your framework with greater ease and integrity?

Closing Words

You have walked far to reach this point. From surveying the land of your inherited beliefs, to sketching the first blueprints of your own framework, to raising its structure and beginning to live within it—you have taken the courageous step of authoring your own path.

As Transient Harmony reminds us, the goal of a conscious framework is not the framework itself. The goal is to reach a place where you can look at what you have built and feel proud—not of the system on the page, but of the **soul you have become** through the process of creating it.

This work is not about completion. It is about appreciation. It is about respecting the path you have traveled, honoring the moments that shaped you, and recognizing the courage it takes to define meaning for yourself.

May you be proud of your framework, but even more so of the person who now carries it.

May you return to these pages again and again—not to meet the same framework or the same self, but to discover a new version of both.

May you grow deeper, clearer, more expansive each time you revisit this journey, knowing that the framework and the soul are unfolding together.

Your framework is alive. So are you.

May the two continue to evolve in harmony, guiding you on this journey of life— and beyond.

SPACE FOR REFLECTION

SPACE FOR REFLECTION

SPACE FOR REFLECTION

SPACE FOR REFLECTION

SPACE FOR REFLECTION